Copyright © 2020 Brittany Scott. All Rights Reserved.

Limitless Me - A Wonderful Tale Of Overcoming Fear

Illustrated by Kimberly Manley

ISBN: 978-1-952779-39-8

Library of Congress Control Number: 2020912696

Acknowledgements

Writing this book has been challenging, but it has also been more rewarding and fulfilling than I ever could have imagined. None of this would have been possible without my best friend and husband, Torrian Scott, who encouraged me and financially supported this project throughout the whole process. I am so blessed to have him by my side.

A special thank you to my children, Landon and Kaylan, who continually asked me, "Mommy, are you done with your book yet?" Their persistence helped me to complete this project. They are my constant inspiration to aim high and reach for the stars.

I am extremely grateful for my parents, Pastors Eric and Caren Susberry, who are my greatest example in life. As a child, when I struggled with fear or failure, they were right there to help lift me up. Their faith and dedication to God has inspired me to never settle for mediocrity, but to live a limitless life that supersedes barriers.

I cannot begin to express my thanks: to my beautiful sisters, Erica Reed and Noel Rey, who always supported me along the way; to my cousin and true friend, Dominique Phelps, who helped me pray this book into fruition; to my friends, Yolanda Willis and Kristen Thorson, who gave me invaluable feedback to help strengthen and expand my story; and, to my former principal, Laura Devine Johnston, whose desire to see all children succeed inspired me to encourage my students to live out their "Limitless Me" potential.

I would also like to extend my deepest gratitude to Jackie Ruiz, Michele Kelly, and the whole Fig Factor team. Their one-on-one guidance, dedication, and positive energy helped me to turn my dream into a reality. Also, to my illustrator, Kimberly Manley, who brought so much depth to my story. What an amazing experience I've had. I am eternally grateful!

Dedication

For Kaylan and Landon. For YOU.
Embrace your world of possibility!

"Hi! I am Faye."

"Today is my day.
Look at my face!
I'm in a good place.
Got faith to believe.
Got faith to achieve.
I'm thrilled to be me.
So happy and free."

Before being free,
there was INSECURITY.
Why? You might say,
did I feel this way?
Let me explain,
what kept me contained.

The School Audition

I was born to act,
that is a fact.
My book of skits,
would one day be a hit.
I loved imagination,
lively narrations,
clever costumes,
and a gorgeous ballroom.
Inventive scene changing,
lots of rearranging.

I could act out each role,
with perfection and soul.
An astounding show,
when I was solo.

The school audition,
was my new mission.
The leading role,
my heart and soul.
Had to try out,
so many doubts.
'Cause with an audience,
fear was obvious.
I was so shy,
filled with butterflies.

"Come on now Faye,"
the teacher did say.
"It may seem quite tough.
You're more than enough.
Come on, don't pout.
Erase the doubt.
INhale, EXhale.
You will prevail!"

So, I stood straight and tall,
wanted to give it my all.

But...
I heard lies in my head.
Oh, what a dread.
"I can't! Uh uh.
I'm not! Uh huh."
Infection had spread.

She hollered, "ACTION!"
I froze, no reaction.
I just mumbled
and fumbled.
Forgot what to say
so, I sat straightaway.

I heard giant snickers,
My sick stomach
felt sicker.

Leah got the role.
That role was my goal.
To be the fairy
would have made me merry.
Instead my role was minor,
a simple two-liner.

**Why did I hide
what I knew
was inside?**

I was thrilled to be me,
but didn't feel free.
Fear of failure and rejection
was my infection.

My Best Friend Jessie

Grew up with Jessie,
had fun being messy.
Free all the time,
for recipes with slime.
Playing for hours,
with our superpowers.
Together forever,
our lifelong endeavor.

Yet that all ended,
couldn't comprehend it.
She had tried out,
So then I was cut out.

No time for slime.
No time to climb.
Things had changed,
we grew estranged.

I must admit,
we no longer fit.
But boy that was tough,
was I not enough?

They said I was dorky, a little bit quirky. Funky fashion was my passion.
Purple pants was my style. Cheetah print made me smile.
But I feared to be weird. So, I just complied, style tossed aside.
I dressed to impress. I changed my hair, and what I'd wear.
But to no avail, it was an epic fail.

The Science Presentation

That friendship thing,
left quite a sting.
Tossed and turned,
feeling concerned.
When I fell asleep,
the alarm clock beeped.
Today was the day,
I couldn't delay.
Had to get dressed,
my hair was a mess.
What could I wear?
My skirt with the flare
was nowhere in sight.
So, I settled alright!
Stuffed my whole face
as I rapidly raced.

"Honey please wait,
you left your display!"
"Come on now, Faye,"
my mother did say.
"It may seem quite tough.
You're more than enough.
Erase the doubt,
don't you dare pout.
INhale, EXhale.
You will prevail!"

But...
I heard lies in my head.
Oh, what a dread.
"I can't! Uh uh.
I'm not! Uh huh."
Infection had spread.

Presentation on whales didn't go so swell. Broke my display.
Forgot what to say. Mumbled and fumbled, then sat straightaway.

The rest of the week was, ummm, kind of bleak. I looked at my grade,
was truly dismayed. I'd tried and failed, I didn't prevail.
Why did I hide what I knew was inside? I was thrilled to be me,
but I didn't feel free. Fear of failure and rejection, was my infection.

Lunch and Recess

Favorite time of day, now felt sad and gray.
Lunch and recess made me stressed.
Feeling alone, was in my zone.
Thinking of the past. Why didn't it last?
Clearly in a funk, a funk that really stunk.

Until I heard contagious laughter,
made my sadness slowly shatter.
Zappy, wacky, chatty, fun!
Fun for each and everyone.

They were confident, that was evident.
Each was different, yet, no predicament.
Seemed relatable, maybe compatible.
They were wonderful, and very colorful!

I dreamt of FRIENDSHIP. A perfect blend-ship.
No need to prove, or to be approved.
No need to act, in order to attract.
A pact like that would be great.
But wait! Their pact, seemed jam-packed.
Was there room for me to bloom?
Plus... What would I say?
I could just say, "Hey!"
They'd probably just stare, wondering why I was there.

I heard lies in my head.
Oh, what a dread.
"I can't! Uh Uh."
"I'm not! Uh huh."
Infection had spread.

So, I walked away.
Perhaps another day.
Why did I hide,
what I knew was inside?

I was thrilled to be me,
but I didn't feel free.
Fear of rejection,
was my infection.

"You're more than enough!"
Those thoughts in my head.
I lay in my bed, it's true what they said.
I've got to believe, I can't be deceived.
My thoughts were so deep, I drifted off to sleep.

The Dream

I dreamt I was pushed in a box. Like a rabbit, being led to a fox.
I screamed, I kicked, I ran, I flipped. I fought so hard, I almost tripped.
Then, I gave up, didn't fight anymore. I was tired and hot, and oh so sore.
Reluctantly, I was pushed in the box. Secured and taped, what's my escape?

Ok, here's my chance.
Gotta get into my fighting stance!
Here I go,
no more doubt.
Then I heard a voice shout.

"Wait, wait, play it safe,
cause you're in a new place.
Don't act out in haste,
maybe danger awaits."

"Danger," I said, "Who are you
to know that?"
"Please help! It is tight, and my
legs are all cramped.
I can't see, it is dark.
Oh My Gosh! It is damp."

"No, no, play it safe, just stay there, if you dare.
For if you stay there, you'll be treated with care.
Here's a pillow, a blanket, a light, and some food.
I even have music, if you're in the mood."

So, I thought, and I thought...

"What would you do?
Would you play it safe too?
I need some advice. Yes, I'm talking to you!
Would you take the chance, without even a glance?
What if it's good, but the unlikelihood.
I hope it is good. Will I cope if it's not?
So many ifs, fear is making me stiff!"

Then I heard another voice inside me say.

"Believe in yourself, believe you are great.
Believe you are better, don't take the bait,
even if you're unsure of your fate.
It's better to hope in what you can't see,
'cause being confined limits all you can be."

"So, take a chance, leap into faith.
Don't stay, wait, or play it so safe,
because outside the box,
maybe great things await."

Ok, I'm convinced. I'm about to break free.
I'll take some deep breaths,
and count to three.
1……..2…….. 3……..

"Thank you! That is so true.
I don't mean to stare, but who is that over there?
I love her gown and her sparkling crown.
Is she in a play?"

"Yes, a play on Broadway. As a matter of fact,
she's the leading act."

"I'd love to see her show. Can we sit in the front row?"

"She is strong, courageous
and very vivacious.
I love every moment,
and every component."

"What is her name
and her claim to fame?"

"Did she ever have fears,
over the years?
Did she ever fail?
What did that entail?
Did she always believe,
or were there tricks up
her sleeve?"

"Hi Faye!
Glad you enjoyed the play.
I overheard your questions
about what led me in this direction.
Well… I believed in me,
and what I could be.
Changed my stinkin' thinkin,'
then I was set free."

"What was your process?
How did you progress?
And what's next for you?"

"Well look inside,
I'll give you a clue."

"Hey, Faye, it's time for your next show."
"Ok here I come. Look, I've gotta go."

"So, you're Faye too? Wait, who are you?"

"That's for you to decide! Remember! Toss fear to the side."

That's when I woke and fear broke.
I was no longer timid me, because I had an epiphany.

"You see, box material is just what I'm not. I'll rip it, I'll break it,
I'll tear it in two. I'll stomp it, I'll shred it, I'll break out, it's true!
I'll ship it, I'll snip it, I'll make an airplane, or two. A car, a school bus,
I don't care what I do. Just so long as I'm not inside of it. True!
This box is about my size. It is safe, I'd fit comfortably, too,
but it'd put so many limits on what I can do."

"Now! Take a look at you,
admire the view,
and let these words ring true."

"I'm thrilled to be me,
and now I feel free.
Fear of failure and rejection,
no longer my infection."

"I will not hide
what I know is inside."

"'Cause Limitless Me, makes me feel free!"

Limitless Me, embraces a world of possibility!

"Limitless Me" exists inside of you.
Yes, YOU!
A world of possibilities await.
Are you ready to climb the endless beyond-the-clouds staircase?

Reflection Questions

You're not Box Material. You're Limitless Me.
What insecurities do you have? What fears do you have? How can you overcome those insecurities and fears?

Failure Happens. Try Again!
What have you failed at? How can you overcome your failures?

Change your Stinkin' Thinkin'.
What do you love about you? What makes you unique? What are your gifts and talents?

Say it. Think it. Believe it.
What are you saying about yourself? What are some good things you can start saying about yourself?

True Friendship. A Perfect Blend-ship.
What are the qualities of a good friend? Who would you consider to be good friends in your life? Why? What qualities make you a good friend?

About the Author

Brittany Scott challenges people of all ages to live out their own "Limitless Me." Her motivation comes from childhood experiences, as there were times she struggled with self-doubt and fear. Over the years she has overcome those barriers through prayer, changing her perspective, speaking positivity into her life, and believing beyond her limitations.

She loves to share her story, and encourage others to climb the endless, beyond-the-clouds staircase to a world of possibilities along with her. She believes that with faith, nothing is impossible. If you believe, you can achieve more than you could ever imagine!

A lifelong learner and educator, Brittany is a member of the Society of Children's Book Writers and Illustrators. She received her B.A. in elementary education at the University of Illinois, and went on to obtain her masters' degree in curriculum and instruction at Concordia University. She also has an English Language Learning Endorsement from Saint Francis University.

Brittany taught elementary education for seven years, was an adjunct professor, and is currently a business owner, teacher, speaker, and writer. She was born in Chicago, Illinois, and is happily married with two children.

Made in the USA
Columbia, SC
09 April 2021